Play Piano with...
COLDPLAY

Wise Publications
part of The Music Sales Group

London / New York / Paris / Sydney / Copenhagen / Berlin / Madrid / Tokyo

Published by
Wise Publications
14/15 Berners Street, London W1T 3LJ, England

Exclusive Distributors:
Music Sales Limited
Distribution Centre, Newmarket Road,
Bury St. Edmunds, Suffolk IP33 3YB, England
Music Sales Pty Limited
20 Resolution Drive, Caringbah, NSW 2229, Australia

Order No. AM979132
ISBN 1-84449-336-9
This book © Copyright 2003 by Wise Publications.

Compiled by Nick Crispin.
Music arranged by Paul Honey.
Music processed by Paul Ewers.
Cover designed by Michael Bell Design.
Cover photograph courtesy of London Features International.
Printed in Great Britain.

CD Recorded, mixed and mastered by Jonas Persson.
Lead and backing vocals by Jo Edwards.
Piano by Paul Honey.
Guitars by Arthur Dick.
Bass by Paul Townsend.
Drums by Brett Morgan.

Your Guarantee of Quality
As publishers, we strive to produce every book to the highest commercial standards.
The music has been freshly engraved and the book has been carefully designed to
minimise awkward page turns and to make playing from it a real pleasure.
Particular care has been given to specifying acid-free, neutral-sized paper made from
pulps which have not been elemental chlorine bleached.
This pulp is from farmed sustainable forests and was produced with special regard for the environment.
Throughout, the printing and binding have been planned to ensure a sturdy,
attractive publication which should give years of enjoyment.
If your copy fails to meet our high standards, please inform us and we will gladly replace it.

Amsterdam

Words & Music by Guy Berryman, Jon Buckland, Will Champion & Chris Martin

Guitar Capo 1st fret

1. Come on,___ oh

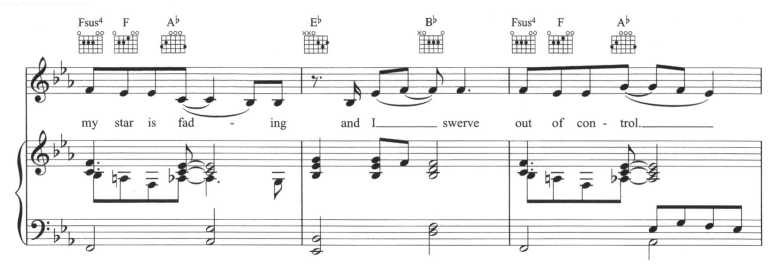

my star is fad - ing and I___ swerve out of con - trol.___

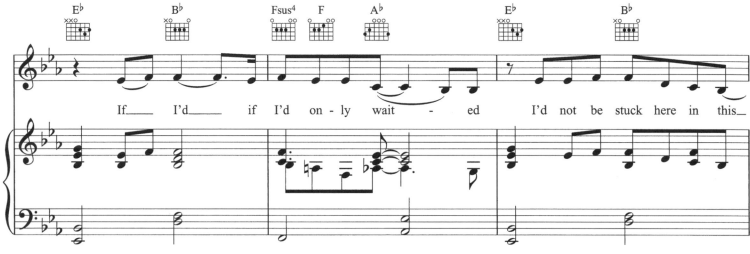

If___ I'd___ if I'd on - ly wait - ed I'd not be stuck here in this__

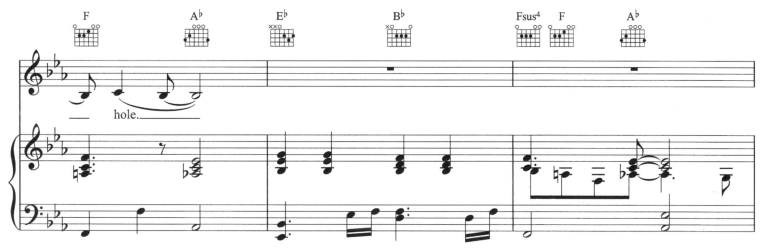

___ hole.___

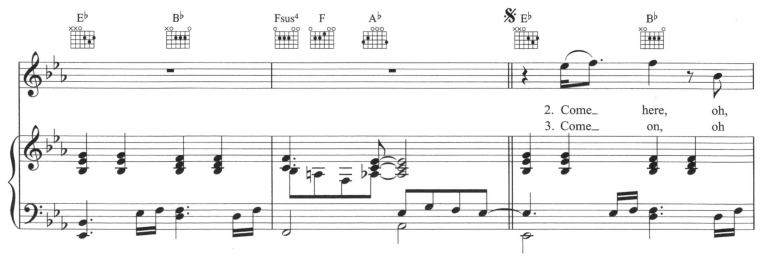

2. Come___ here, oh,
3. Come___ on, oh

my star is fad - ing____ and I_____ swerve out of con - trol.____
my star is fad - ing,____ and I_____ see no chance of re - lease____

____ And I_____ swear I wait - ed and wait - ed.____ I've got to get out of this____
____ and I_____ know I'm dead on the sur - face, but I am scream - ing un - der -

____ hole.____
- neath._____ But time is on your side,____

____ it's on your side_____ now._____ Not push - ing you down____

7

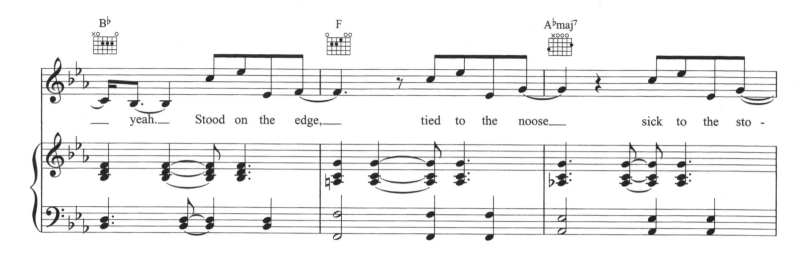

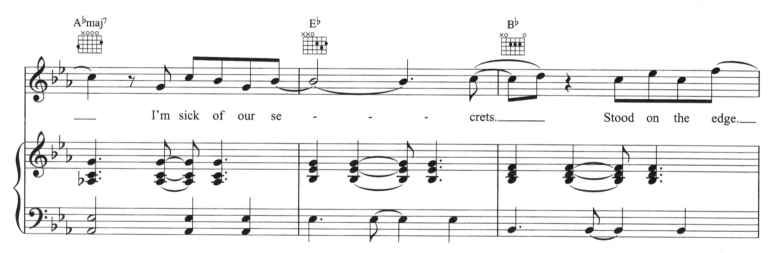

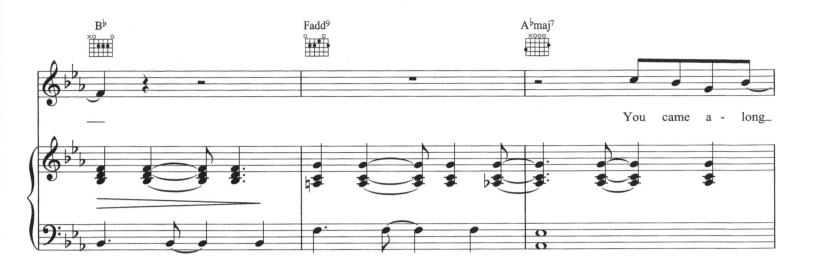

You came a - long ___

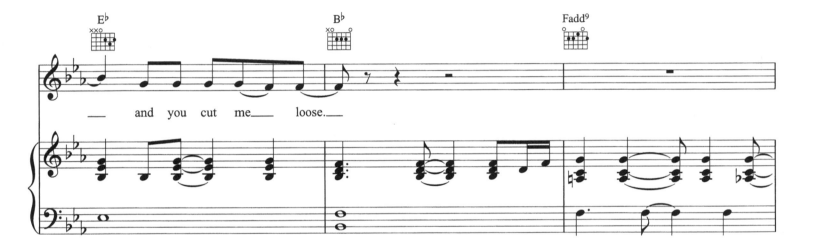

___ and you cut me ___ loose. ___

You came a - long ___ and you cut me ___ loose. ___

Clocks

Words & Music by Guy Berryman, Jon Buckland, Will Champion & Chris Martin

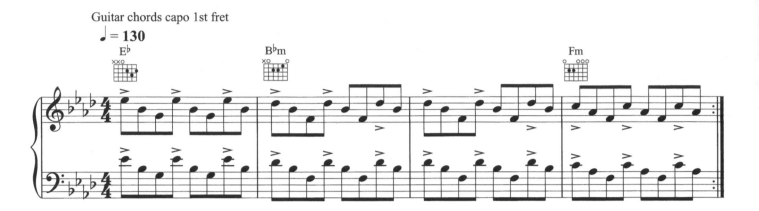

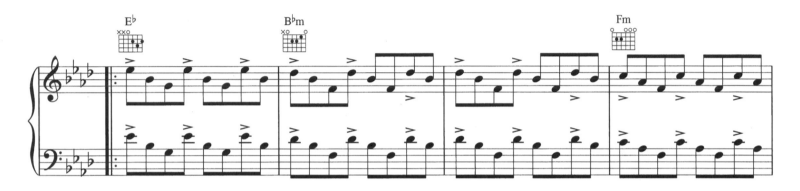

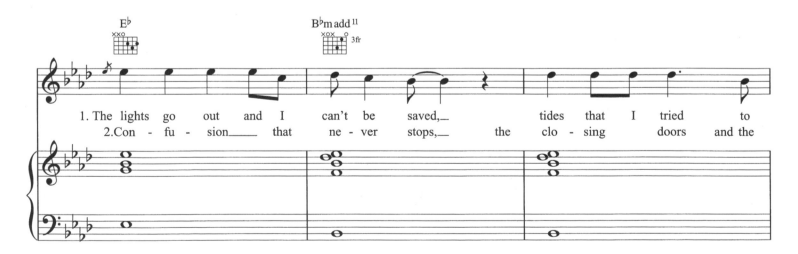

1. The lights go out and I can't be saved,___ tides that I tried to
2. Con - fu - sion___ that ne - ver stops,___ the clo - sing doors and the

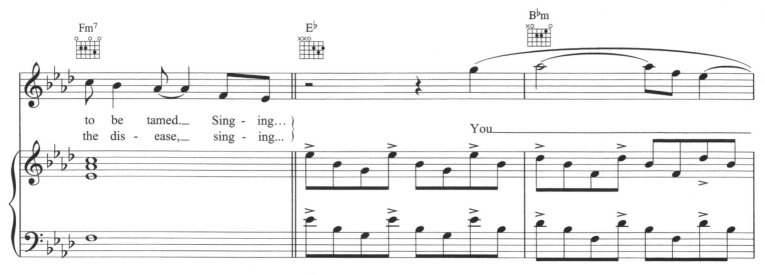

to be tamed.__ Sing - ing...

the dis - ease,__ sing - ing...

You_____

__ are._____

You____

_____

are.____

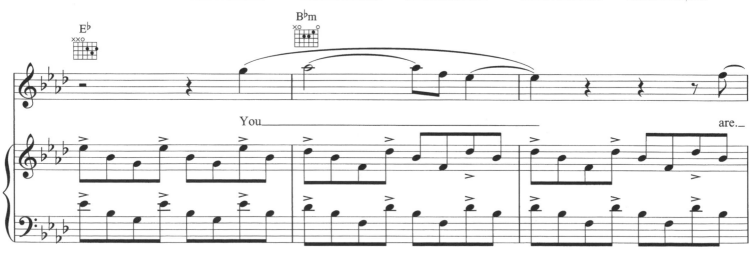

You_____

are._

12

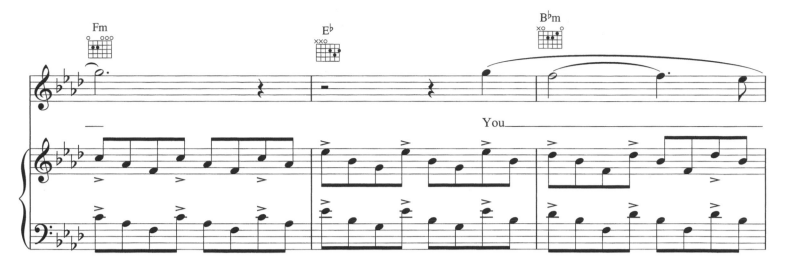

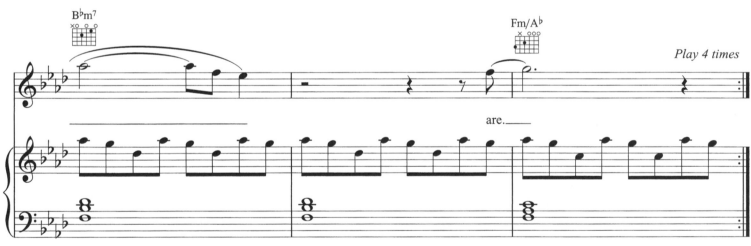

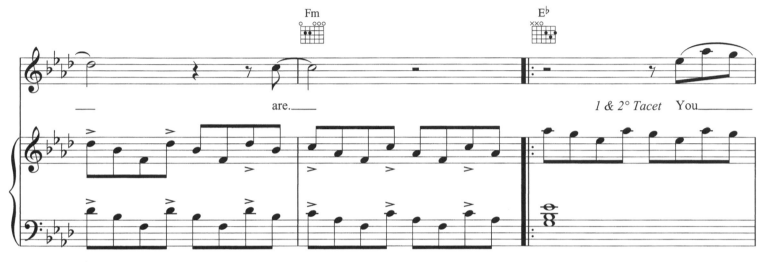

And no - thing else com - pares.

And no - thing else com - pares.

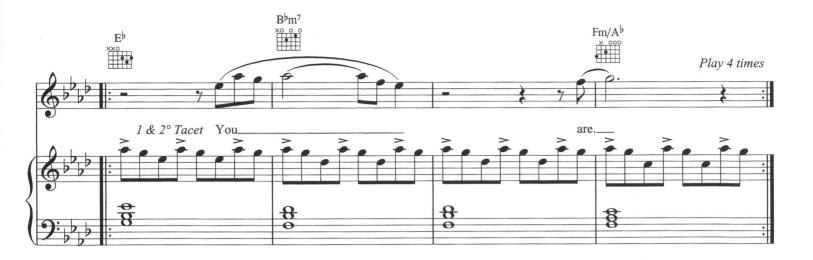

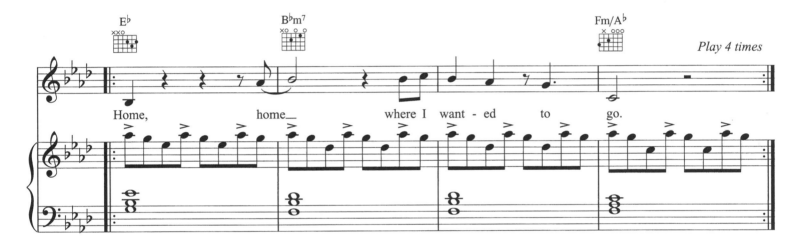

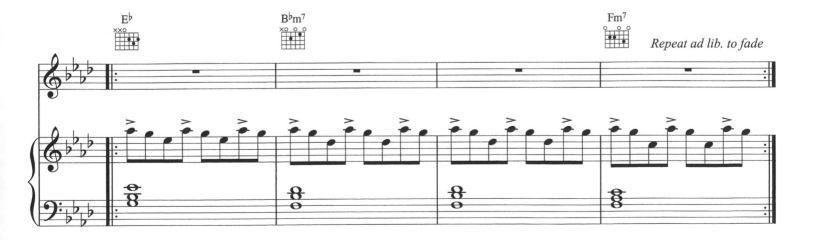

Everything's Not Lost

Words & Music by Guy Berryman, Jon Buckland, Will Champion & Chris Martin

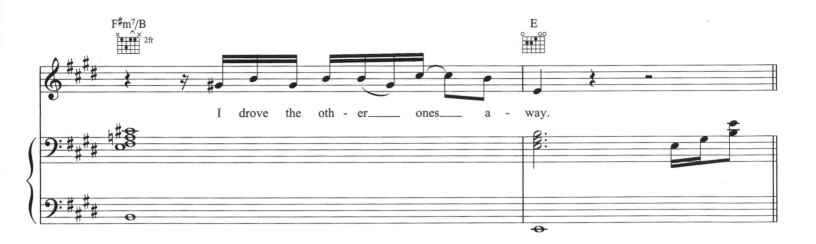

I drove the oth-er___ ones___ a - way.

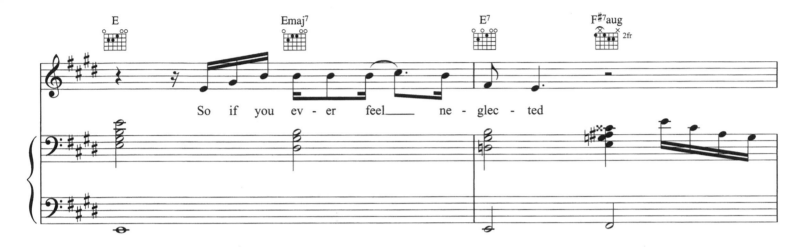

So if you ev - er feel___ ne - glec - ted

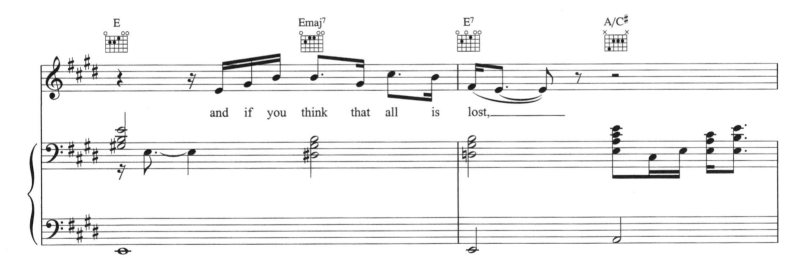

and if you think that all is lost,___

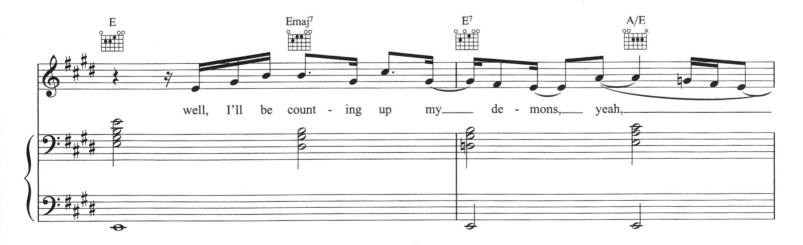

well, I'll be count - ing up my___ de - mons,___ yeah,___

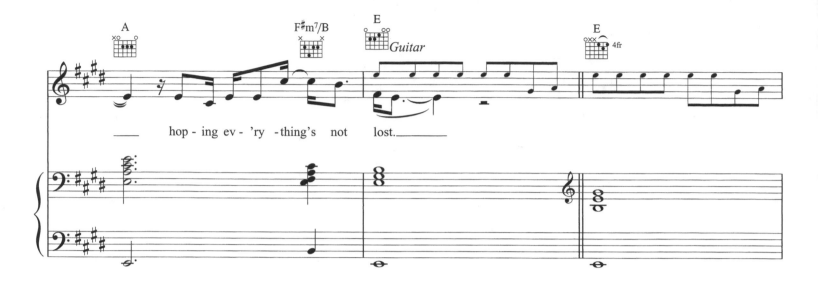

hop - ing ev - 'ry -thing's   not   lost._____

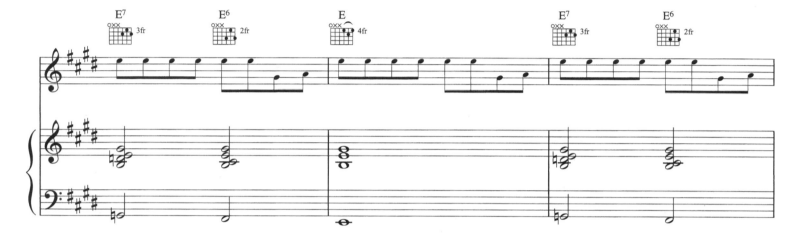

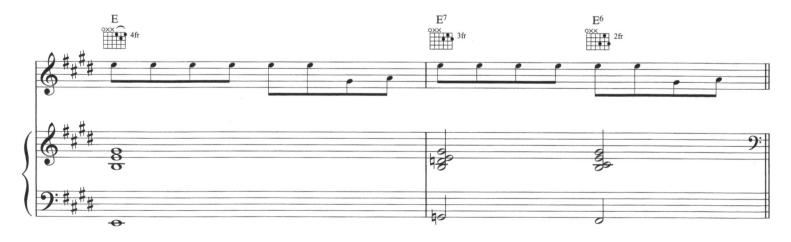

well, I'll be coun - ting up my_____ de - mons yeah,_____

_____ hop - ing ev - 'ry - thing's_____ not lost.____

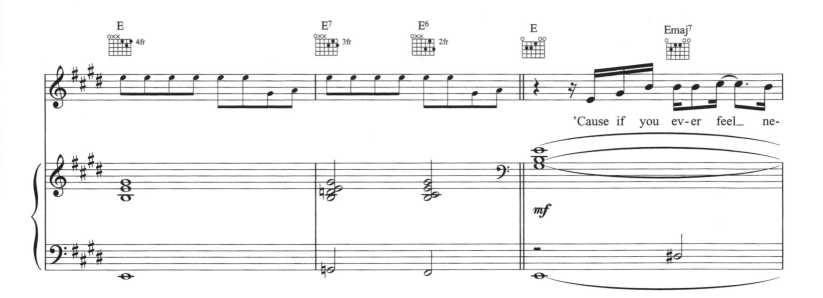

hop - ing ev - 'ry- thing's___ not lost._____ Sing - ing

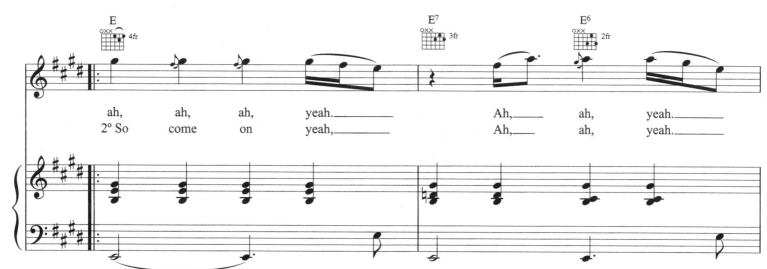

ah, ah, ah, yeah._____ Ah,___ ah, yeah._____
2° So come on yeah,_____ Ah,___ ah, yeah.

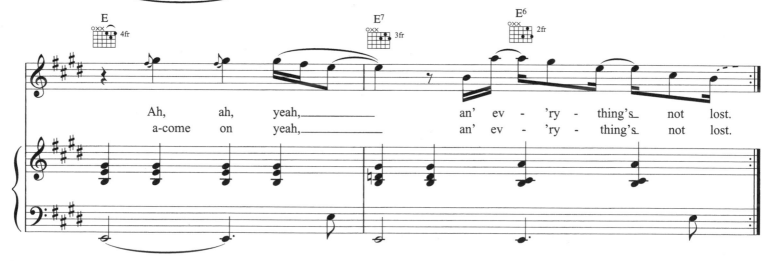

Ah, ah, yeah,_____ an' ev - 'ry - thing's___ not lost.
a-come on yeah,_____ an' ev - 'ry - thing's___ not lost.

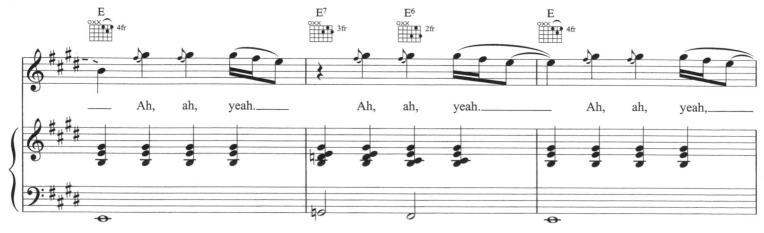

___ Ah, ah, yeah._____ Ah, ah, yeah._____ Ah, ah, yeah,___

22

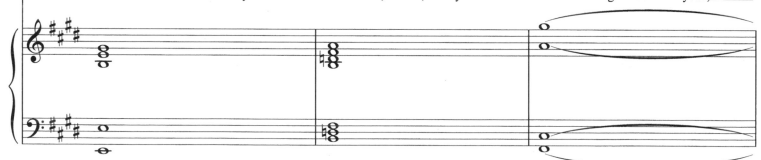

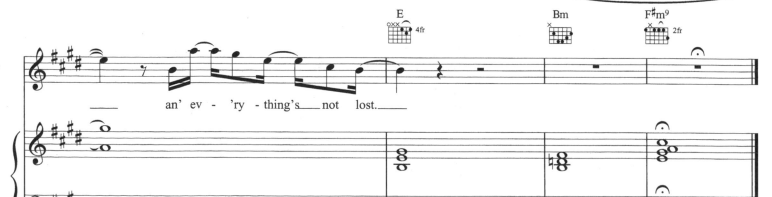

Politik

Words & Music by Guy Berryman, Jon Buckland, Will Champion & Chris Martin

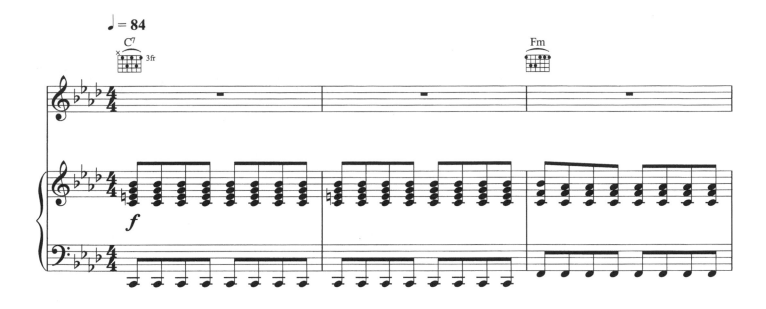

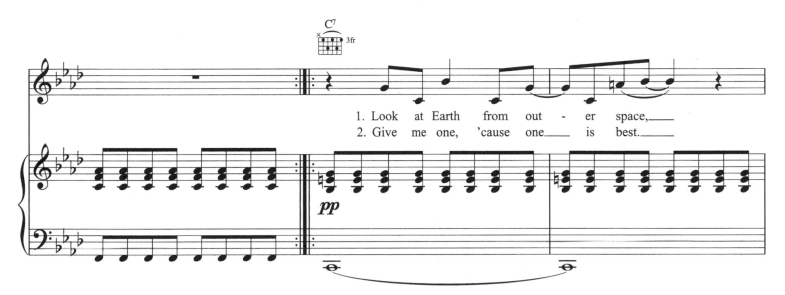

1. Look at Earth from out - er space,
2. Give me one, 'cause one is best.

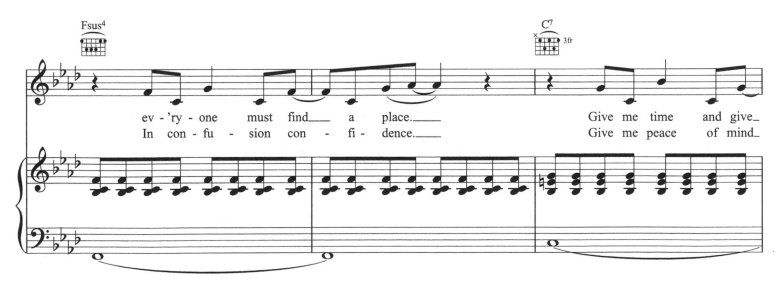

ev - 'ry - one must find a place.
In con - fu - sion con - fi - dence.

Give me time and give
Give me peace of mind

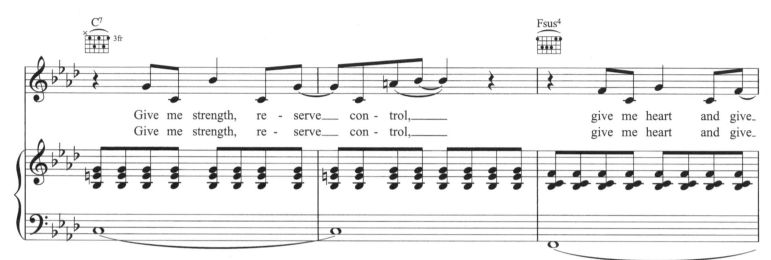

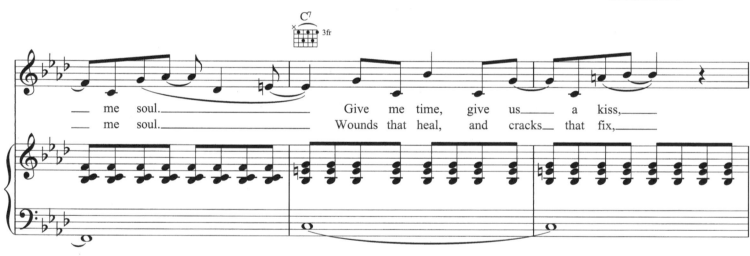

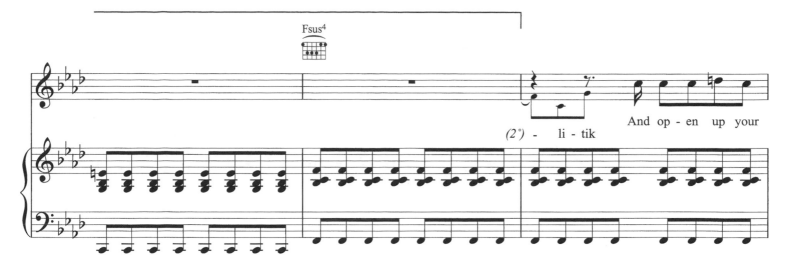

Fsus⁴

And op - en up your

(2°) - li - tik

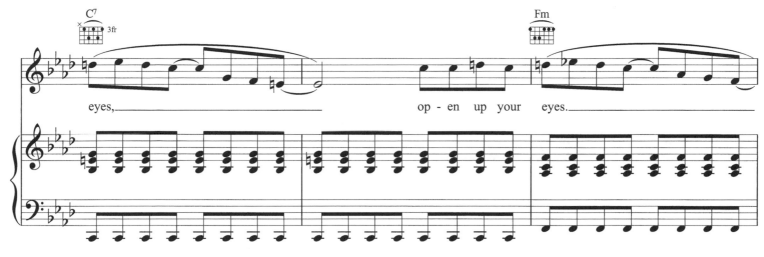

C⁷   3fr

Fm

eyes,_____   op - en up your   eyes._____

C⁷   3fr

Op - en up your   eyes,_____   op - en up your

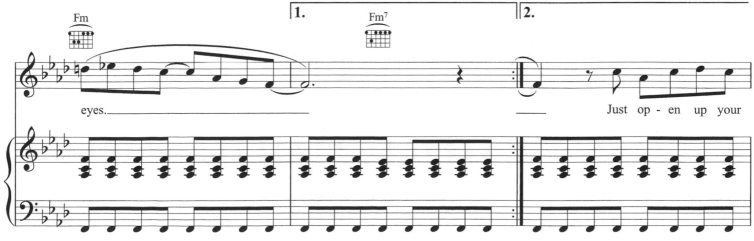

Fm

1.   Fm⁷   2.

eyes._____   Just op - en up your

27

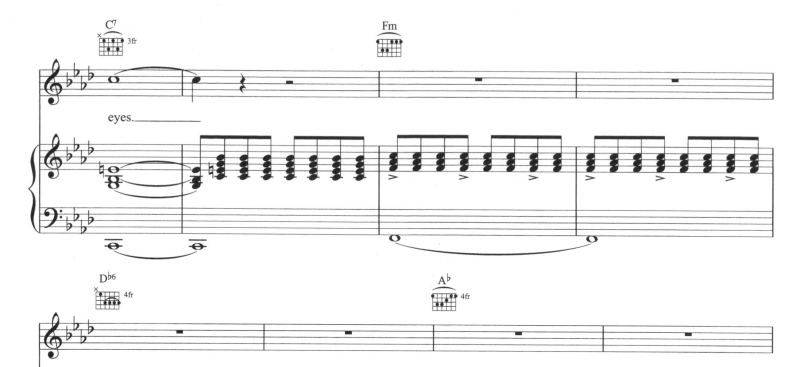

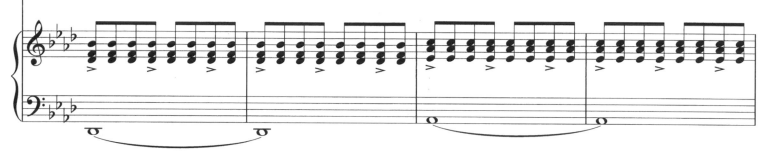

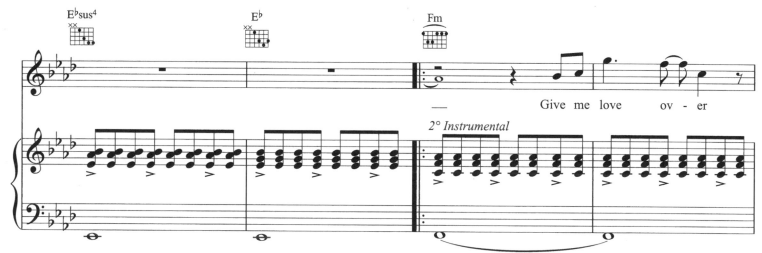

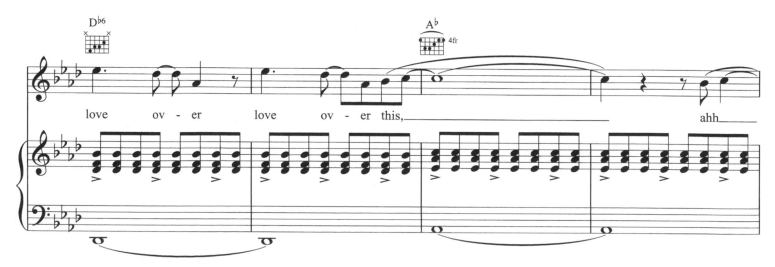

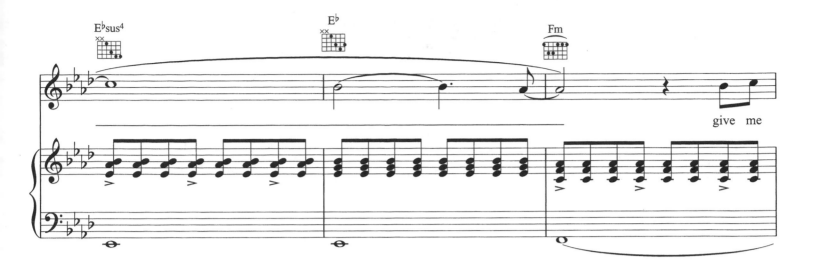

give me

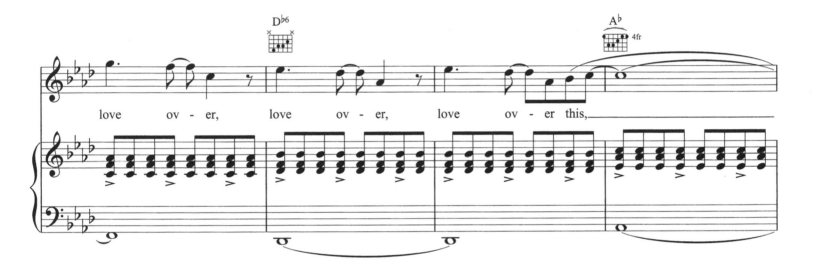

love ov - er, love ov - er, love ov - er this,___

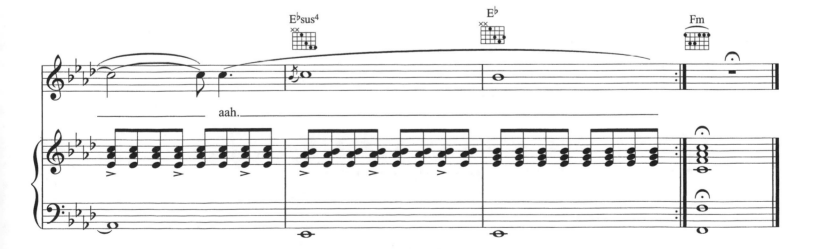

aah.___

The Scientist

Words & Music by Guy Berryman, Jon Buckland, Will Champion & Chris Martin

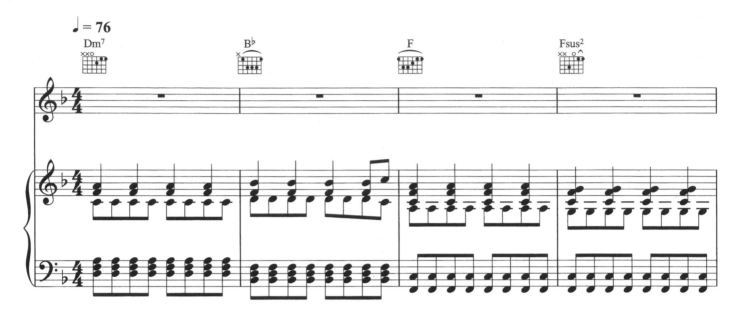

1. Come up to meet___ you, tell you I'm sor - ry, you don't know how love-
2. I was just guess - ing at num - bers and fig - ures, pull - ing the puz -

-ly you are._____ I had to find___ you, tell you I need_
-zles a - part._____ Ques-tions of sci - ence, sci-ence and pro -

___ you, tell you I'll set____ you a - part._____ Tell me your sec-
- gress that must speak as loud___ as my heart._____ Tell me you love_

-rcts and ask me your ques-tions, oh, let's go back to the start._____ Run-ning in cir-
___ me, come back and haunt_ me, oh and I rush to the start._____ Run-ning in cir-

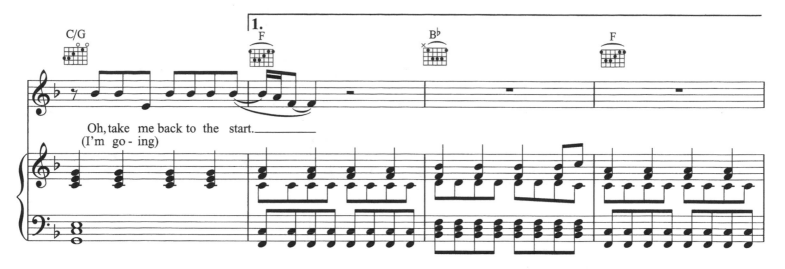

Oh, take me back to the start.
(I'm go - ing)

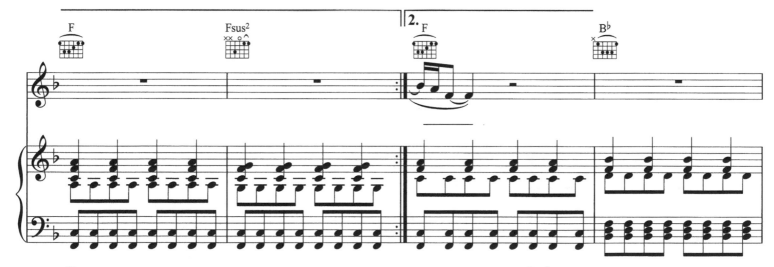

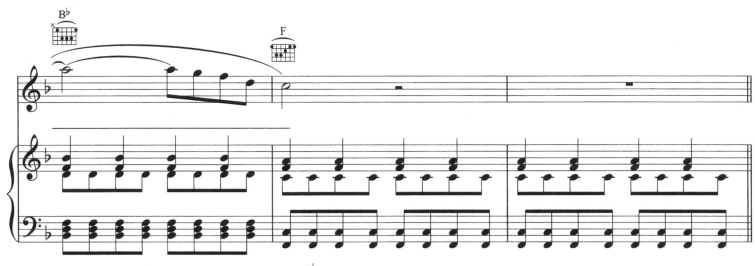

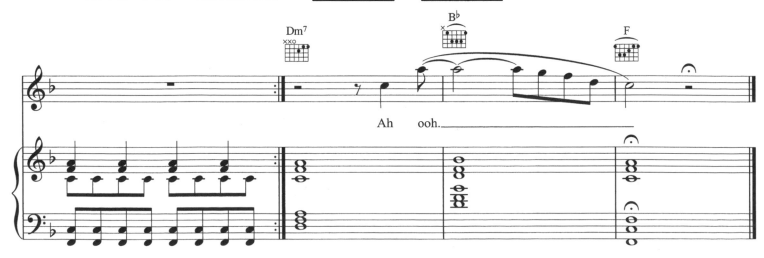

Trouble

Words & Music by Guy Berryman, Jon Buckland, Will Champion & Chris Martin

and thought of all the stu-pid things I'd said.

2. Oh no, what's this? A spi-der web and I'm caught in the mid-dle.
3. Oh no, I see, a spi-der web and it's me in the mid-dle.

So I turned to run, and thought of all the stu-pid things I'd
So I twist, and turn, but here am I in my lit-tle bub-

done.
ble. Singing out, ah,_____ I nev - er meant to cause you trou - ble.____ And

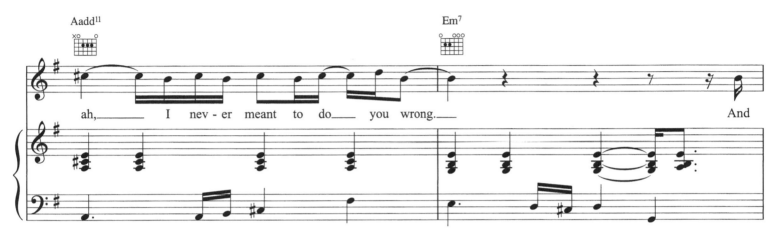

ah,_____ I nev - er meant to do____ you wrong.____ And

ah,_____ well if I ev - er caused____ you trou - ble,____ then

To ⊕ *Coda*

oh no, I nev - er meant to do____ you harm.____

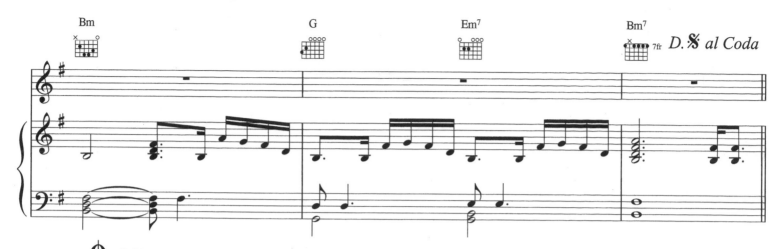

CODA

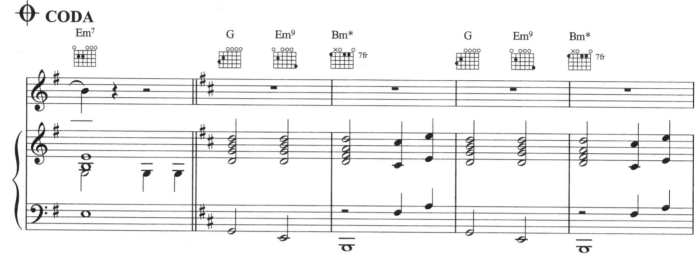

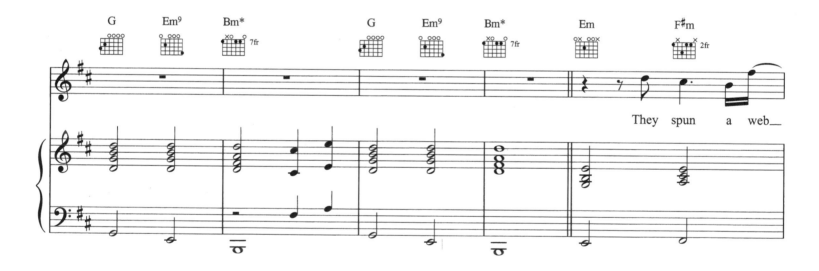

They spun a web___

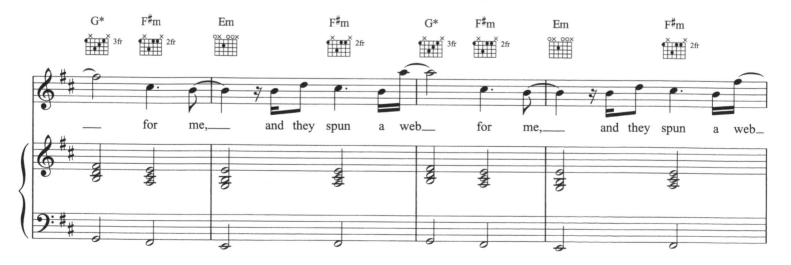

___ for me,___ and they spun a web___ for me,___ and they spun a web__

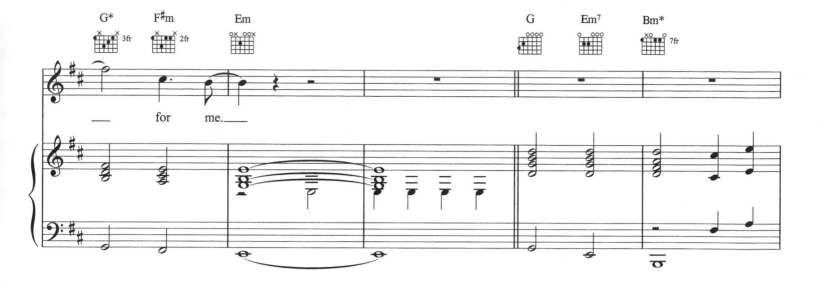

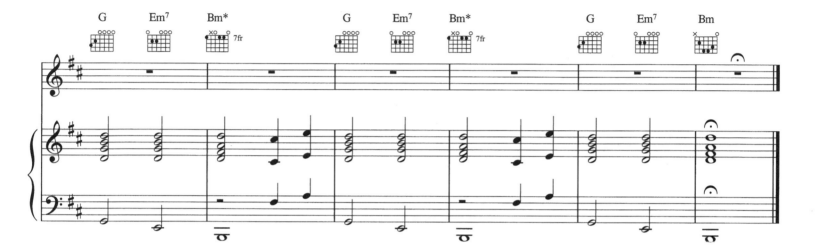

CD Track Listing

Full performance demonstration tracks...

1. Amsterdam
2. Clocks
3. Everything's Not Lost
4. Politik
5. The Scientist
6. Trouble

Backing tracks only (without piano)...

7. Amsterdam
8. Clocks
9. Everything's Not Lost
10. Politik
11. The Scientist
12. Trouble

All tracks: Berryman/Buckland/Champion/Martin
BMG Music Publishing Limited.